MW01047996

# Education on the Internet

• • • • • • •

# A Student's Guide

• • • • • • •

*1997 Update*

By Andrew T. Stull

Adapted for Merrill Education by

**Randall J. Ryder**

Merrill,
an imprint of Prentice Hall
*Upper Saddle River, New Jersey    Columbus, Ohio*

Editor: Debra A. Stollenwerk
Developmental Editor: Carol S. Sykes
Production Editor: JoEllen Gohr
Director of Marketing: Kevin Flanagan
Advertising/Marketing Coordinator: Julie M. Shough
Design Coordinator: Karrie Converse
Production Manager: Patricia A. Tonneman
Electronic Text Management: Marilyn Wilson Phelps, Matthew Williams, Tracey
    Ward

©1998 by Prentice-Hall, Inc.
Simon & Schuster/A Viacom Company
Upper Saddle River, New Jersey 07458

This publication was adapted by Randall J. Ryder for Merrill Education from *Life
on the Internet: Biology, A Student's Guide*, written by Andrew T. Stull to accompany
*Biology: Life on Earth*, by Audesirk & Audesirk, ©1996 by Prentice-Hall, Inc.

Printed in the United States of America

ISBN: 0-13-889999-1

**TRADEMARK INFORMATION:**
*America Online* is a registered trademark of Quantum Computer Services Incorporated. *CompuServe* is a trademark of CompuServe, Incorporated. *Netscape Navigator* is a registered trademark of Netscape Communications Corporation.
*Prodigy* is a registered trademark of Prodigy Systems Incorporated. *Astound* is a
registered trademark of Gold Disk. *Eudora* is a registered trademark of QUAL-
COMM Enterprise Software Technologies (QUEST). *Internet Explorer* is a registered trademark of Microsoft Corporation. *PowerPoint* is a registered trademark
of Microsoft Corporation.

The author and publisher of this manual have used their best efforts in preparing this book. The author and publisher make no warranty of any kind,
expressed or implied, with regard to these programs or the documentation contained in this book. The author and publisher shall not be liable in any event for
incidental or consequential damages in connection with, or arising out of, the
furnishing, performance, or use of the programs described in this book.

# Contents

• • • • • • •

# Introduction
# O Brave New World
• • • • • • •

## *Brief Internet History*

There are important things that history can teach you. If you don't learn them then you may find yourself walking into problems or even trouble that otherwise could have been avoided. Don't get me wrong, there is a lot of junk out there that is called history, but take a look at it first before you decide you don't really need it.

This thing that we now call the Internet has been around for just over twenty-five years and has been changing in a dynamic manner. Its age is irrelevant for our discussion here, but the reasons for its creation and growth are quite interesting and helpful in understanding its nature, its terminology, and the culture of the people that have adopted it as home.

The Internet has been likened to jello pinned on a wall: its form and size constantly changing. In reality, the Internet is a combination of computers linked together, or a network of computer networks. In the late 50's and early 60's, scientists and engineers realized the importance of using computers to share information. Initially, voracious computer networks used a variety of these computer protocol languages. And only those that shared a common language could communicate with one another. The Internet evolved in an effort to create a network that would use a common language. Initially, the U.S. government paid for the development of a common network communication language which was readily adopted world wide.

There is no central Internet agency and therefore the Internet is independent of governments and regulation. It grows and changes from the common need and commitment of the people who use it.

If you saw a map of this global network you might easily recognize it as an irregularly shaped fishing net. Despite its seemingly chaotic distribution, the network provides users the advantage of easily connecting between any two points. This vast connection of computers is called the "Internet" and it was born in 1969. Although the Internet is still used for

1

scientific purposes, its use in the home and schools has exploded in recent years. Today, in the United States, over 22 million people connect with the Internet from home, and over 7 million connect from school.

The Internet has evolved to meet the demands of its users. Although its initial purpose was to allow a distributed system for scientific exchange and research, it gradually took on the role of digital post office (electronic mail and file transfer). As technology changed, the transfer speed and the way we viewed the information changed. Earlier work on the Internet relied on a "command-line interface," where a user simply typed commands from a keyboard and waited for the response. DOS-controlled computers are an example of this. Recent advancements have brought us the graphical user interface (GUI). Macintosh and Microsoft Windows are classic examples of systems that use a GUI. These GUIs rely on icons and images to symbolize activities and commands. Actions are initiated with a mouse click instead of a typed command. One of the first commonly used GUIs for the Internet was *Gopher*, developed at the University of Minnesota in 1991. The title *Gopher* comes from the fact that UM's mascot is the gopher. If you have spent any time around computers, you may have noticed that computer hacks have a fondness for rodents. Actually, they have a fondness for cartoons and old movies too. When you get a chance, see if you can find the services *Archie*, *Veronica*, and *Jughead*.

*Gopher* is a visual tool for the Internet, where information is presented as a hierarchical listing of directories and files. The users jump from general directories at higher levels to more specific directories at lower levels until they find what they want. Beyond searching for information on a single computer, *Gopher* allows the users to quickly and transparently jump from one computer to another. This method of interaction no longer requires the users to log on to each computer independently but rather allows them to wander or *browse* (the *Gopher* people call this process "burrowing") at will among the vast stores of information on the world's computers. Once the information is found, it can easily be downloaded to the user's computer. By simplifying the access to and use of the Internet, the number of users and businesses has increased at astronomical rates. It's amazing if you think about it! You could be on your computer in Toledo, Ohio, jumping from one screen to another and without realizing it you might find yourself in Hamburg, Germany, Mexico City, or Tokyo, Japan. Wham! And no airline tickets!

The next major tool for the Internet followed in 1989 when Tim Berners-Lee created the World Wide Web (Web) at CERN's Internet facility in Switzerland. Although *Gopher*, as an initial attempt at navigating the Internet, was a good GUI, its "text only" appearance was mundane and lacked the power of visual components. Now, with the introduction of the Web, users could traverse the Internet to access text,

2

visual images, video, and audio presentations in a manner that was easy to navigate and that included colors.

Information on the Web is posted as a "page," which may contain text, images, sounds, and videos. The organization of a page is much like any printed page in a book. There are the visual improvements but the major innovation is the use of *hypertext*. Hypertext is the use of words *and* images as links or connecting points to different text, images, sounds, or videos on other computers throughout the world.

After the introduction of the Web, there was a dilemma: a great place to go but no easy way to get there. Kind of like the moon in the 60s. The one thing still lacking was a convenient program which would allow users to access the Web easily. This program, called *Mosaic*, was developed in 1993 by the National Center for Supercomputing Applications (NCSA). Not only did *Mosaic* allow for the browsing of Web pages, but it added the ability to use other Internet resources such as electronic mail, *Gopher*, and a means to transfer software programs. Since the release of this browser, the Web has been growing at a phenomenal rate. In 1991, there were around 700,000 Internet users. Following the introduction of *Mosaic* in 1993, the number increased to around 1.7 million. In early 1997 the estimate was more than 45 million. Today, the Internet is becoming a daily fixture in our everyday lives as we connect to the Web for such tasks as previewing movies, booking airline flights, observing radar and satellite images, listening to cuts of new audio CDs, and even doing our shopping. But the best is yet to come! Soon, the Internet will monitor our home appliances, provide us the means to purchase "electronic books," and allow us to tailor the information we want delivered to our computer automatically. So hang on to your socks. Our trip into cyberspace may just knock them off!

# Chapter 1
# The Basics of Moving About the Internet

•••••••

## *Navigation Strategies*

Using the Internet is a lot like beginning to drive a car. At first, most of your attention is directed at the various actions and behaviors that are required to move your vehicle through traffic and avoid various obstacles. But once you acquire the basics of driving, the process becomes more automatic and you can acquire additional skills such as driving a manual transmission or traveling an icy highway. As in learning to drive an automobile, no two individuals normally demonstrate the same level of knowledge of navigating the Internet. Many of you have a lot of experience with computers, while others have none at all. As you read this chapter, you will likely find it helpful to have a computer with an Internet connection available to you. For those of you who have not traveled down this electronic superhighway, there is no need to panic. You will find several resources in the Appendixes to help you get started. These resources include a description of the necessary equipment (Appendix I) and a list of companies that would be glad to help you connect to the Internet for a small fee (Appendix II).

There are numerous software programs that browse the Web, communicate with electronic mail, read newsgroups, and allow video and audio transmissions on the Internet. Until recently, connecting to these Internet resources required the use of multiple programs. Now, however, both Netscape and Microsoft offer packages that contain a suite of programs. These packages allow you to browse the Net, send e-mail, view newsgroups, and connect to Internet phone programs—all within the same software program. While Microsoft's *Internet Explorer* is an excellent program, the examples and screen images in this manual are generated from the *Netscape Navigator* 3.01 software.

## 1.1    What Lies Under the Hood of Your Browser

The software that you'll use to access the Net is commonly called a *Web browser.* This browser on your computer allows you to communicate with your service provider's computer server. Connections to the Web allow the server and your computer to use hypertext mark-up language or HTML. The basic visual element of HTML which your browser displays on your monitor is called a *page.*

So, what really appears on these Web pages? The best way is to see for yourself. If you can, sit down in front of a computer, start your browser software, and connect to the Internet. Your browser is probably already set to start at a specific page. Web pages usually include both text and images displayed in various colors. Some will also use sounds and videos. It is this rich environment of sounds and visual information that provides the multimedia environment of the Web. When you choose a page it will be sent to your computer. After the requested information has been sent by the server, your browser will display it for you. As a basic rule, anything that can be saved or recorded onto a computer can be provided and distributed on the Internet through a Web page.

### Connecting to a Page

While the Internet may appear at first glance to be disorganized, finding your way around can be simplified by learning to use a few powerful navigational features of your browser. Once you become familiar with these features finding your way through the Internet is really no harder than finding your way to a friend's house. Suppose that your friends are having a party at their new house and supplying all the entertainment and food. You're familiar with their town so you need only their address to get to the party. Navigating the Internet with a Web browser is even easier. If you want to go someplace on the Web, all you do is type the address into the browser and connect to the desired page. No map required.

Information on the Internet has an address just as your friends do. Most browsers allow you the option of typing in an address and going directly to that document. With *Netscape,* there are two easy ways to do this. The easiest way is to use the *Open* toolbar button. A small window will appear and offer you the opportunity to type in the address of the desired document. A second method, and also one employed by other browsers, is to modify the browser so that Internet addresses are viewable.

With *Netscape,* you can open this window by selecting *Show Location* from the *Options* menu (Figure 1). The address window (see Figure 2) will appear immediately below the toolbar buttons. Just type in the requested addresses and press the return button on your keyboard.

**Figure 1**

Within *Netscape*, the selections under the *Options* menu act as toggle buttons. They can be alternately turned on (with a check mark) or off (without a check mark) by selecting them.

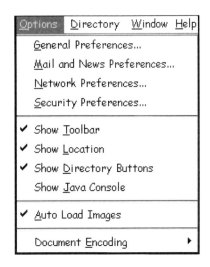

## Imbedded Navigation

You don't always have to know the address of a page to view it. The wonderful thing about the Web is that you can access (navigate) pages through the use of *hyperlinks*. Hyperlinks are a functional part of moving around the Web. You will notice these hyperlinks as colored words on the page. Images may also serve as hyperlinks. Your mouse is used to select or click on the desired hyperlink. Some Web authors write their pages so that their hyperlinks are hidden from you. If you are new, just click on everything. You can't break it.

With recent innovations in writing Web pages, other interactions are possible. Clickable images or maps are becoming a prominent way of interacting with Web pages. With a clickable image, you have the option to select/click a section on the image which functions as a hyperlink. This

**Figure 2**

With the *Show Location* option selected in the *Options* menu, the *Location* window will appear on your browser just below the toolbar.

Now that you know how to do it, here is an important address to get you started. This is the home page for the Prentice Hall text *Internet for Educators* (1997), which contains a multitude of links to Education resources on the Web.

**http://www.execpc.com/~hughes**

by <u>Randall James Ryder</u> & <u>Tom Hughes</u>

ISBN 0-13-239187-2

This site created by Flint Hahn and maintained by <u>Tom Hughes</u>
Copyright © 1995, 1996, 1997. Site last updated: February 13, 1997.

The Java Applet Navigator Ticker developed by <u>ITS of Egypt</u>.

is different from the normal image link because the author of a Web page can connect one image to many different places. An example might be an image of an animal cell. The creator of such a document might place a hyperlink under each picture of the different cellular components so that your selection of different cellular components would take you to different pictures and information.

Here are two addresses that use a clickable map. The first is Virtual Tourist of Central America, and the second is the Exploratorium, an interactive museum.

**http://www.vtourist.com/webmap/cam.htm**
**http://www.exploratorium.edu/**

Not all browsers support clickable maps but most good Web authors will still provide the same choices using conventional hyperlinks.

Hyperlinks are great for navigating the Internet. However, there are many documents that don't incorporate hyperlinks. If you end up on one of these pages, you'll need another method of navigation or you'll be in trouble. This is very similar to driving through a neighborhood, turning the corner onto a dead end, and realizing you don't have a reverse gear. The solution, of course, is to *have* a reverse gear. Netscape's *Navigator* and Microsoft's *Internet Explorer* incorporate a Back, Forward, and History feature to allow you to hop back and forth to recently viewed pages. The Back button takes you to the previous screen. The Forward button moves you ahead to the next screen (presuming that you have moved back a page or more). The History option is a super cool feature. It keeps track of all the Web sites (specific locations) that you have visited during your present on-line session. By clicking on any of the sites you have visited, you are automatically returned to that site without having to enter an address. This process is described in more detail in the next section.

Although I'm using illustrations of the *Netscape* browser to illustrate points for the manual, you'll find that most browsers differ in appearance only to the degree that their toolbar buttons for basic navigation are in different order (something you can handle). Figure 3 illustrates the basic orientation of the navigation buttons for *Netscape Navigator.*

One of the most useful features you'll have is the *Home* button. This feature allows you to jump, just like Dorothy with her ruby slippers, back to your beginning page. We'll discuss later in the manual how to choose and set this page. Two additional buttons that are common on most browsers are the *Reload* and *Stop* buttons. *Netscape* also includes many

**Figure 3**
The *Netscape* Navigator 3.01 Web browser offers a wide selection of basic navigation and control buttons at the toolbar. This is a representation of the control strip from the Windows version, but the Macintosh version is quite similar in function and similar in appearance. The toolbars from other browsers offer similar functions.

other features within its toolbar to give you flexibility in navigating the Internet, but they are self-explanatory and may differ from some of the options provided by other browser programs.

Use one of the addresses presented in this chapter or, if you want to take a look at an index of Web sites, try the following:

**http://www.yahoo.com/index.html**

*Yahoo!* is a directory of information that originated at Stanford University. Remember: You won't break anything and if you get lost, you can always shut down the program, have lunch, and try again later!

Up to now, everything on a Web page has been described as a point, click, and jump. A new feature called *Forms* has added an entirely new dimension to both the user and the creator of Web pages. On some Web pages, you will find a section where you may be asked to give information by typing from the keyboard. This information might be in the form of a user survey, an answer to a question, or a request by you to a Web server. An example of the use of forms is the *BrainTainment Center* home page that contains a number of intelligence tests that you can complete on-line, then have your results displayed within a matter of seconds.

Experiment with some of the various assessment devices on the *Brain-Tainment Center* and amaze your friends and colleagues with your intellect! Don't take the results too seriously. After all, it is just an on-line test that purports to predict a narrow aspect of intelligence.

**http://world.brain.com/**

## 1.2   Using Web Addresses

The addresses that you've been using on the Web are called Uniform Resource Locators, or URLs for short. Each URL has a couple of basic parts just like a residential address. Look at the URLs (now you know what they are called) listed below. Note the similarities in these addresses.

**http://www.microsoft.com**
**http://www.ariel.co.uk/sagent**
**http://www.psychicpicks.com/**
**http://www.intellicast.com**

---

Here is yet another example of a typical URL and a pretty cool site in itself. There are three basic components to a URL. Compare this with the others I've given to you.

**http://sln.fi.edu/tfi/hotlists/hotlists.html**

Here are the three components:

| | |
|---|---|
| **protocol** | http:// |
| **server** | sln.fi.edu |
| **path** | tfi/hotlists/hotlists.html |

---

It may seem confusing at first, but think of it as nothing more than a postal address squished together without any spaces. The various components of the URL denote how the information is stored. In the address below, "http" refers to the protocol or language form which all Web servers speak. The colon and slashes are used to separate it from the name of the server. They are not always present with every type of URL. The path www.msnbc describes the location of the Web page on the server.

**http://www.msnbc.com**

The last part of the server name (in this case, .com) defines the domain to which the server belongs. A domain is just a fancy name for a functional network group. The most common domain that you'll see is the .edu domain that encompasses educational institutions.

One more thing, just so you can't say that I didn't tell you. In your travels, you will eventually jump to a server that is outside your country.

Some of the other domains you are likely to encounter are *com, gov, mil, net,* and *org.* Here are a couple of examples that you might be interested in. Can you determine what their domain represents?

**http://aol.com**
**http://www.nps.gov/**
**http://navysgml.dt.navy.mil/patteam/wwwintro.html**
**http://envirolink.org/**

Much, but not all, of the information on these servers is in English (so unless you are paying attention you might never know your foreign whereabouts). URLs of foreign servers have an additional section at the end of the server's name. It is a two-letter code that denotes the country. Here are just a few examples, but I trust that you can find more:

| | |
|---|---|
| .au | Australia |
| .ca | Canada |
| .ch | Switzerland |
| .nl | Netherlands |
| .pe | Peru |
| .uk | United Kingdom |

## Bookmarks

One you begin to amass a bunch of web sites you will need a way to index or store the URLs so you may easily return to the site without having to enter the entire address. This is where bookmarks come in. You bookmark the web site to which you wish to return. Just to get your collection started, try this address:

**http://www.hotwired.com**

It's the on-line version of *Wired* magazine and a pretty interesting place. If you like their page, you can save a bookmark by selecting *Add Bookmark* from the *Bookmarks* menu on your browser (Figure 4). Now, if you use your mouse to go back to the *Bookmarks* menu, you'll see that *hotwired* is just a jump away. You don't have to memorize the URL and you don't have to haphazardly jump around until you find it again.

Newer browsers provide the option of organizing your bookmarks in categories. Additionally, as shown in Figure 4 it is possible to save your bookmarks on a disk so you may transport and use them on another computer. This is a great way to share bookmarks with others and have access to your bookmarks as you use different computers.

Up until this point, we have only been discussing browsers as an interpreter for documents that use hyperlinks. However, browsers also have the power to link to other, much older, formats of information that is available on the Internet. Let's look at two different URLs. The first is an FTP site, or a location where you will find a directory of files you can download to your computer. The second type of URL is a *Gopher* site which is limited to text displayed in black and white. Links to multiple FTP and *Gopher* sites can be found at the following location:

**http://www.execpc.com/~hughes/links.html**

I'm sure that most of you have done this, but just to catch the loose ends I'd like the rest of you to visit the following site. This Web page of *Yahoo!* contains a hyperlinked random generator designed to randomly drop you on a URL somewhere in the world. Simply click your mouse on the "random" icon at the top of the page and you will be connected to a site.

**http://www.yahoo.com**

While you are out in the world, see if you can find URLs from other countries. Remember that you can always use your Back or Home button to return to the safety of home.

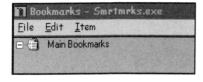

**Figure 4**

After you've added bookmarks to your browser they will appear in a list under the *Bookmarks* menu on the menubar. Once you've selected a list of bookmarks you may use the *View Bookmarks . . .* to arrange and organize them into categories.

13

## Travel History

If you've been working along with your manual and your browser at the same time, you've probably been to many places on the Web. Obviously, if you want to move back and forth between your selections you are probably using the Forward and Back buttons on the browser's toolbar. But what do you do if you want to go back to someplace you've visited fifteen jumps ago? Do you press the Back button fifteen times? Well, you could, but eventually that process would become tiresome. Computer hacks are lazy sometimes and using the Back button fifteen times would drive them crazy. There's a great feature that allows you to jump rapidly to any of the places you've visited along your path of travel. If you are using the Netscape browser, click on *Options* and you'll see a list of all of the places you've visited on your journey (see Figure 5). Other browsers have similar features. The simple point is that if you don't want to use the Back button fifteen times, you can select from a list of recently viewed pages.

---

Now that you've got the hang of it, give the following URLs a try. There are a wide variety of Web sites here, so feel free to explore and find something of interest.

**http://espnet.sportszone.com/**
ESPN Sports: Lots of information, scores, news and interviews with sports figures.

**http://www.foxnetwork.com/home.html**
FOX Broadcasting Company: What's playing on FOX.

**http://www.mapquest.com**
Mapquest: Maps, maps and more maps!! Plan a trip or personalize maps for your needs.

**http://www.whyfiles.news.wisc.edu/**
The Why Files: Very cool place to gain a deeper understanding of science and technology.

**http://www.npr.org**
National Public Radio: Listening guides and audio files that you can download.

**http://pathfinder.com/**
Time Warner Communications (*Life, People, Sports Illustrated,* and more)

Remember, when you find something of interest, save it to a bookmark!

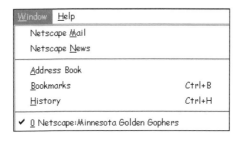

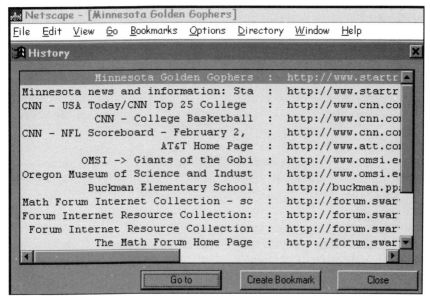

**Figure 5**
The History option allows you to see where you have been and provides you an easy way to return to sites observed previously during an on-line session.

•••••••••
## Activities
By this point you have had the opportunity to get a good sense of what a Web page looks like and how you can navigate to various sites. To provide you some additional practice with connecting to a site and to allow you to gain a better understanding of the global nature of the Web, try the following activities. The only thing that you'll need to engage in these activities is the knowledge of reading URLs and saving bookmarks.

### All the News on the Web
In this activity you will tour various worldwide news sources on the Internet. You will find a comprehensive set of links listed on

15

**http://www.trib.com/news/**

For each *news source* you connect to, note (1) its URL, (2) the content of the site, and (3) the country in which the site is located.

## Becoming a Cyber-Tourist

This exercise provides you the ability to be a global tourist using cyberspace. You will quickly become acquainted with new places, things of interest, and people. If you find something that you like, set a bookmark or record the URL so that you can return to that site at another time. Once you connect to the Virtual Tourist at

**http://www.vtourist.com/**

note (1) the number of countries and regions within a country that have Web sites, and (2) the variety of languages that are used on these sites. Enter this URL, then explore the world on the Virtual Tourist.

## Generating Bookmarks

Creating bookmarks is an important skill to acquire. Over time your travels on the Web will provide you a plethora of rich and powerful resources that you will want to visit again and again. Creating bookmarks allows you to connect to these sites rapidly and efficiently. Also, if you place your bookmarks on a diskette, you can transport your personal bookmarks from one computer to another. Later on in this book you will learn how to set up bookmark files. For now, connect to the starting point for all the government's websites:

**http://www.www.fedworld.gov**

As you proceed to various links, capture each site by placing it on your bookmark file. Later on in the book you will learn how to organize these bookmarks. But for now, just try to accumulate sites under your bookmark menu.

# Chapter 2
# Caught in the Net

## • • • • • • •

## *Education Resources*

In Chapter 1 you learned what the Internet is, how to use a browser, and what resources are available to you through the Web. If you have devoted some time now to examining the content of the Internet, in this chapter you will learn about the various "goodies" that are available to you on the Web (such as graphics, sound, video, etc.). And you will learn how to use some very powerful software and Web sites that will search for information. These search engines and software programs that serve as search agents provide teachers the ability to access information that would have been unheard of just a few years ago. Finally, this chapter will present you with Web resources that can be used in an educational setting. Furthermore, within this chapter, you will learn a number of tricks for using these search engines.

## 2.1   So What Kind of Stuff Is on the Web?

Teachers need to have access to a lot of information to facilitate students' learning. In the past, educators have relied upon the content of textbooks and supplemental printed materials. While convenient, these sources often contained information that was dated and presented it in a manner that may not have reflected the most current thinking about educational practice. As our society increasingly focuses on one's ability to both acquire and make sense of information, there will be an increasing emphasis on this skill for our students. Recognizing that information comes in various forms, you will examine a variety of hypertext resources on the Web presented in the form of graphics, text, audio, video, and downloadable software.

- **Graphics**
  The Web contains graphic information in a variety of forms, including photographs, drawings, computer-generated art, and live images that are captured with digital photography and pre-

sented in the form of a motionless image. Here is an annotated list of just a few sites containing a variety of graphic images:

**Weathernet**

**http://cirrus.sprl.umich.edu/wxnet/**

A rather amazing site! Here you will find color and black-and-white photos and satellite imagery of weather formations throughout the world. The site also displays recent radar images of any location in the United States.

**World Museums**

**http://www.lam.mus.ca.us/webmuseums/main.shtml**

This is the Natural History Museum of Los Angeles County site that contains links to hundreds of museums throughout the world. It also contains links to three other museum indices: Nedsite List of Museum Indices, World Wide Arts Resources, and World Wide Web Virtual Library.

**Virtual Hospital**

**http://www.vh.org**

Not for the faint hearted. This site presents graphic images of various parts of the body and the effect of various diseases on body organs and tissues.

Images on the Web can be saved and reproduced in various forms. The most simple procedure to save an image is to print it as it is being displayed on your monitor. This process will vary according to the type of operating system your computer uses so check your operating system user manual for specific directions on printing from your screen. A second form for saving images is to save them on your hard drive or a fixed disk. Again, the process for saving screens (also called screen dumps) varies with operating systems, so again check your user manual. Once saved on a file, however, these images can be inserted into word processing documents, presentation software such as Microsoft's *PowerPoint* or Gold Disk's *Astound,* or they can be printed on your color or gray scale printer.

- **Text**
  Clearly there is a considerable source of information on the Web available in text format. In fact, some sites actually allow you to download sizeable files. There are a variety of sites that are rich resources to locate text on various topics. Among these sites are libraries, sites that contain on-line periodicals and journals, and entire books. Again, here are a number of sites offering a variety of information in the form of text.

**Library of Congress—Internet Resource Page**

`http://www.loc.gov`

Hundreds of text documents from the legislative, judicial, and executive branches of government as well as documents from foreign governments, states, and the military.

**Project Gutenberg**

`http://gutenberg.etext.org/`

Complete version of hundreds of books. Here you can download *The Red Badge of Courage, Peter Pan, The Scarlet Letter, A Tale of Two Cities,* and other great classics.

Text can be saved or edited in a variety of ways. The most direct process is to save the text using the save command from your browser. If you use *Netscape,* simply go to the top of the screen, click on FILE and then select "save as". The program will then ask you for a name to assign to the file and where you would like to view the file. Once saved, you can examine the file by clicking on the name of the file in the directory where it has been placed. Once you have selected this file, *Netscape* is activated (even though you may not be on-line) and the file can then be viewed just as though you were connected to the Web although everything you view on your screen is actually information saved on your computer. Another procedure to save text is to use your mouse to click, then highlight the text displayed on your screen. Next, go to the top of the screen, click on EDIT and COPY the file. It has now been saved on your clipboard and can be pasted into your word processing program. Finally, text can also be obtained by downloading text files from FTP sites. One of these sites, Project Gutenberg, allows you to download hundreds of complete books.

- **Audio**

   The Web can act as a radio station, a telephone, or a cassette player. If you have a sound card installed in your computer you can "listen" to live broadcasts, talk with people around the world (at no cost), and download sound files that can later be played. Using these tools requires special software that can be downloaded at no cost. For more information on the use of this software and its capabilities, connect to the following Web sites.

**RealAudio**

`http://www.realaudio.com`

This site explains uses of the RealAudio player and directs you to sites where you can listen to on-line audio broadcasts. The software you need to play audio on the Net can be obtained at this site.

**Netscape**

**http://home.netscape.com/comprod/products . . . ator/version_2.0/plugins/audio-video.html**

Netscape maintains a great list of audio and video plug ins that will also work with *Internet Explorer*. At this site you can download copies of such popular audio programs as RealAudio by Progressive Networks and Apple Quicktime by Apple Computer. All programs can be downloaded from this site.

*Internet Phone* **by VocalTec**

**http://www.vocaltec.com**

Yes, you can reduce long distance charges if you and the party you wish to speak to have a copy of *Internet Phone* and a sound card. This site explains the use of *Internet Phone* and allows you to download the free software version.

- **Video**
Yes, the Web allows you to receive video in black and white as well as color. You can also broadcast video on the Web in black and white with the use of a very small camera that can be purchased for less than $100. While the quality of the video is not as good as your television, this is a rapidly developing aspect of the Web. Undoubtedly, the use of video on the Web will advance rather quickly. Information on using video can be obtained from the following sites.

*CU-SeeMe*

**http://cu-seeme.cornell.edu/**

Here you will find detailed descriptions of the use of the *CU-SeeMe* software and links to download the software. By attaching an inexpensive camera and activating this software, you will have the capability of broadcasting almost real time video around the world in black and white or color.

- **Software**
Wow! There is a tremendous amount of software available on the Web. Quite literally you have access to hundreds of thousands of software programs that can be downloaded to your computer's hard drive or fixed disk. Many are educational software designed for classroom instruction. This software is available for numerous operating systems such as Windows, Macintosh, OS-2, and DOS. The most efficient means of locating and downloading software is connecting to the site

**http://www.shareware.com**

which will direct you to over 170,000 software programs. Connect to this site and select the browse command to see the most popular programs, or use the search command to locate software that would be useful in your classroom.

## 2.2   Let Your Fingers Do the Walking

Because the Web is an information jungle, locating that information can be a challenge. The locational tools that I'll describe here are free and easy to use, but you should remember that searching for information on the Internet or elsewhere is a skill that needs to be practiced.

There are three types of tools that are particularly useful in searching for information. These are directories, search engines, and search agents.

### Directories

Directories are sites on the Web that have indexed information similar to the table of contents of a book. *Yahoo!* (http://www.yahoo.com) and AltaVista (http://altavista.digital.com) are two of the many useful directories that are available on the Internet. Indexes are good places to start to get a sense of the diverse types of information that are available, and to become more familiar with moving around to various Web sites. Generally, you will find that an index is a good place to find general topics of interest.

*Yahoo!* is a listing of information by category—kind of like a card catalog. At the top of the listing there are several very general categories, but as you move deeper into the directory you'll notice that the categories become more specific. To find information, you simply choose the most appropriate category at the top level and continue through each successive level until you find what you're looking for or until you realize you're in the wrong place. Don't worry, if you get lost you can always use the *Back* button or the *History* option from the toolbar to get back on track.

As an example, suppose you were attempting to learn more about the use and impact of technology in education. Within *Yahoo!* notice that one of the top level categories is Education. After accessing the Education category, you'll notice that it gives a list of many different categories. So, what is your next choice? My choice is Instructional Technology and Training. Because *Yahoo!* cross-references among the categories, you'll find that several related categories will lead you to your desired page.

Much of your success in finding information with this type of tool really centers around your preparation for the search. Often, it is possible to find information on a topic in a category that may at first seem unrelated to your topic of interest. Again, let's take the example of technology in education. Although you may consider this to be a topic to be searched out from a category in Education, there are other avenues to consider. For example, the category of Science will contain information of the development of technology from a scientific standpoint, and certainly the category of Social Science will contain information on the impact of technology on people and their cultures.

Prepare yourself for a search *before* you jump into one. In the long run it will save you both time and frustration. Don't be afraid to try some strange approaches in your search strategy. A good technique that I use occasionally is to pull out my thesaurus and look up other names for the word. It may be that you can find a more common form of the word. Think of all the associations that your query may have and give them each a try. You never know when it will turn up a gold mine.

## Search Engines

Another more direct approach to finding information on the Web is to use what is called a *search engine*. Don't be confused by the term. It is nothing more than a program that runs a search for you while you're waiting for the results. There are many search engines on the Web. Recently, over a hundred types of search engines have been placed on one site allowing you to readily switch from one search engine to another. This site, called *All-In-One Search Page* (http://www.media-prisme.ca/all/all1form.html), is a useful source for conducting searches on topics, people, spelling, and even quotations. Some of the Web search engines are commercial and they may charge you a fee to run a search. Just as anything that proves itself to be in demand, the Web is turning commercial. You will notice many places will begin as a free service and eventually ask you to pay a fee. Don't worry—there are plenty of free search engines and many more popping up all the time.

One cool search engine is *MetaCrawler* (http://metacrawler.cs.washington.edu:8080). It actually is a search of search engines! That's right. *MetaCrawler* actually searches a number of popular search engines simultaneously, then provides a comprehensive listing of sites that match your search terms. One of the attractions of *MetaCrawler* is that it saves you the time and effort of having to use a number of distinct search engines to conduct a search. Additionally, *MetaCrawler* is pretty fast, which, again, will save you time in the long run. When you first see the opening page, you'll notice that it is very simple. Fear not, behind this page is a very good resource. Reading the instructions on the page will tell you most everything you need to know. Enter a word or phrase into the entry box and press the Submit button; *MetaCrawler* will refer back to its database of information and return a page of hyperlinked resources containing the word you entered. When the query results come back to you, notice that they are hyperlinks to Web sites. Again, by clicking on these hyperlinks you can then go to the site to determine if the information will be of use.

Both as an example of how a search engine works and as a comparison with *MetaCrawler,* use "technology" as the topic for a search using *Yahoo!* (http://www.yahoo.com) and AltaVista (http://altavista.digital.com). Now note the time each search engine requires and the number of "hits" or sites it provides you at the completion of the search. Did you notice that some of your results didn't seem to apply to your topic? If you said yes, then you've noticed one of the downfalls of search engines. They are very fast and very dumb. They don't think (that is your job). A search using the term "technology" is just as likely to turn up a link to a rock band or the name of a commercial establishment as a link to the impact of technology on our society. To perform an effective search you will need to spend time *before* the search preparing a search strategy. When you perform a search using an automated tool like a search engine you can expect many links to be unrelated to your intended topic, but all in all they are very powerful tools that are constantly becoming more efficient.

There is one more way to search for information. Search agents are actually software programs that are separate from your Web browser, but use the Web to search for information. In other words, you can use a search engine without having to activate your Web browser. You will still need to connect to the Internet. But once you have made your connection you start the search agent program, which in turn cruises the Web to locate the information you have requested. Two very efficient search agents are *WebCompass 2.0* produced by Quarterdeck Corporation (http://www.quarterdeck.com) and *Autonomy* (http://www.agentware.com). Both of these programs can be downloaded for a free 30-day trial. Here is a closer look at *WebCompass 2.0* to provide you a better idea of how search agents may be used.

*WebCompass* is extremely easy to use. To search for a given topic you simply enter a descriptor, then wait as the agent goes about searching for the information on the Web. The screen presented in Figure 6 shows an example of the results of a search on "functional literacy." There are several notable elements to the result of this search. First, note the detail of the content that is provided in the results window. For each site located, the program provides the site's URL, the number of links and images contained in the site, and a comprehensive summary of the site's content. The results of a search conducted on *WebCompass* are saved to your hard drive so you may examine the results at any time. You may also delete the results of a search at any time. Finally, once you have made a TCP/IP con-

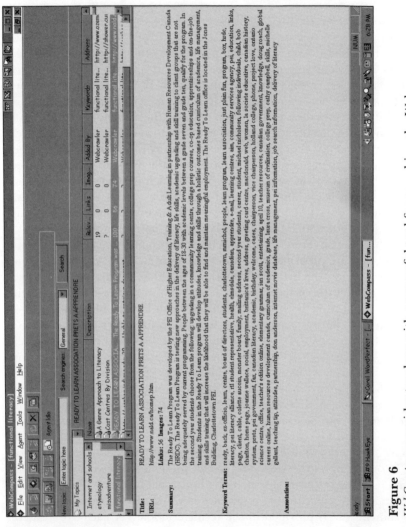

**Figure 6**
*WebCompass* provides teachers with a powerful tool for searching the Web and then providing a comprehensive description of a site's content.

24

nection with your service provider you can start the *WebCompass* program, and by clicking on any of the sites displayed in your results window the program will connect you with that site! Note the advantages of this program in a classroom where you have limited access to the Internet. Results of searches can be examined off-line, the teacher is provided a thorough description of a site's content, and the teacher or student can cut and paste the URLs into a bookmark file. Thus a teacher can effectively create an "electronic card catalog" that also allows students to access the information at a given site simply by clicking on the site's name.

---

With all of the experience that you've accumulated, why don't we put it to a test? Here are some important topics in education. Using your Web browser, connect to *MetaCrawler* or *AltaVista,* and then conduct a search on these topics. Once you have the results, consider how many of the "hits" provided would appear to be useful. You may consider refining your search by using terms that are more descriptive to see if that produces more relevant results.

| | |
|---|---|
| School Finance | Inclusion |
| Cooperative Learning | School Reform |

---

• • • • • • • • •
## Activity

### The Great Cyberspace Hunt

Here's what you've all been waiting for! I've been keeping my ear close to the ground listening for information on education in the popular press and media. The first list is a set of education-related terms that have become popular. See what you can find on these topics. Try to find the information in the least number of jumps possible. How are each of these terms influencing the human condition?

| | |
|---|---|
| Zone of Proximal Development | Cooperative Learning |
| Advance Organizers | Constructivism |
| Information Processing | Metacognition |
| Multiple Intelligences | Schema Theory |
| IDEA (Individuals with | Misconceptions |
| Disabilities Education Act) | Inclusion |

In addition to the terms listed above, I've included a list of education researchers and theorists from this century. Some of them may be easier to track down than others. It has been a very interesting experience for me just to find the right people to include. I hope you'll find both their research and their lives interesting.

Your assignment is to put together a brief history of each education researcher or theorist and their important contributions to education. If you'd really like a challenge, try to draw a thread of connection between each to the others, no matter how thin or obscure. (Hint: To help you understand the challenge task, you should search out the term *Concept Map*.)

| | |
|---|---|
| David Ausubel | Howard Gardner |
| Jerome S. Bruner | John Goodlad |
| John Dewey | John Nussbaum |
| Rosalind Driver | Jean Piaget |
| Elliott Eisner | Louise Rosenblatt |
| Robert Gagné | Lev Vygotsky |

Remember to use all of the resources at your disposal. Begin with the *Yahoo!* Directory and *AltaVista* search engine; then move on to some of the others that are provided in the *All-In-One* search group. Check the obscure as well as the popular resources.

# Chapter 3
# Getting More Out of Your Browser and the Web

●●●●●●●

## *Advanced Techniques*

The information in the first two chapters of this book has provided you with a glimpse of the rich and varied resources that are available on the Web. As you gain more experience using search engines, search agents, and Web indexes you will begin to accumulate a rather extensive knowledge of how to navigate the Web. In this chapter you will learn some techniques to speed up that navigational process, ways to communicate with others on the Web, and finally how you can create your very own presence on the Web. Specifically, you will be looking at some of the options you can use to configure your browser, how to communicate with others through the use of e-mail and newsgroups, and two ways to make your own personal page on the Web.

---

So that you have something for comparison, here are the home-pages for the two most prominent Web browsers, *Netscape* and the Microsoft *Internet Explorer*. They are free if you are a student or work with a school. Within these pages you will also find the manuals for each program.

*Netscape*
**http://home.netscape.com/**

Microsoft *Internet Explorer*
**http://www.microsoft.com**

---

## 3.1   I Prefer It <u>My</u> Way!

The problem with the Internet is time. Too much stuff to look at and not enough time to see it all. Fortunately, there are a number of steps you can use to enhance your browser's performance. With *Netscape,* under the *Options* menu (Figure 7) you are allowed several choices to customize the appearance and function of your browser. Let's take a look at some of these options to determine how they may save you time and allow you to access information in a manner that better suits your needs.

---

The following is the URL for the *Netscape* handbook. You should refer to it whenever my ramblings stop making sense to you. You will also find other resources that will help you so don't hesitate to give it a look.

**http://home.netscape.com/assist/support/client**

---

Examining the *Options* menu, notice that there is a check mark by some of the options. Look at *Auto Load Images* as an example. When the check is present, images will be automatically loaded. If you select this option again, the check mark disappears and subsequently pages will load the text without the time-consuming graphic images. Give it a try. Depending upon the speed of the connection you have with the Internet, you have likely noticed that some screens require a long time to download to your computer. Particularly annoying can be the numerous adver-

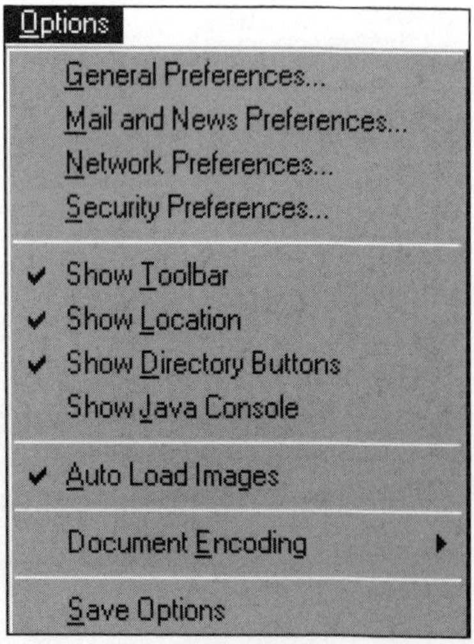

**Figure 7**

Many of the general options are listed in the *Options* menu on *Netscape,* but if you wish to do a more detailed configuration, you can find more options under the *Preferences . . .* submenu.

| Options |
| --- |
| General Preferences... |
| Mail and News Preferences... |
| Network Preferences... |
| Security Preferences... |
| ✔ Show Toolbar |
| ✔ Show Location |
| ✔ Show Directory Buttons |
| Show Java Console |
| ✔ Auto Load Images |
| Document Encoding ▶ |
| Save Options |

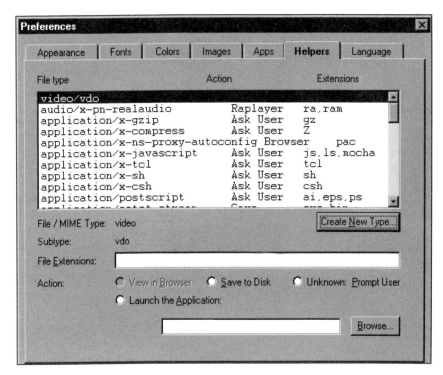

**Figure 8**
There are many choices available to you from within the *Preferences* submenu.

tisements that increasingly are being presented at the top and bottom of your screen. This is not likely to be a major issue if you are going to examine just a few screens, but if you need to travel to numerous sites, all of which have multiple screens containing a lot of graphics, this can become a very time-consuming process. Using the options in your browser, turn off the auto-image function. You will find that your access time will increase significantly. And if there is a particular graphic image you desire, then simply turn the image function back on.

If this isn't enough control for you, there are other changes you can make. Notice the *Preferences . . .* submenu under *Options* (Figure 8). When you select this, you will be presented with a dialog window where you can make even more customizing options. If you don't like the way the font, color, or style of the text appears on your browser, you can change them within this dialog window. Browsers typically provide you with many features to allow you to change the visual appearance of the information on the viewed page. This is a particularly important feature if you want to print an image on the screen in grayscale. Using the color option, you can lighten the background color to

obtain more contrast in the image you print. (You will find that it is very difficult to print an image that contains text against a dark background color.)

After opening the *Preferences* . . . dialog window, you will notice a
couple of words in a box near the top of the window just to the left of a
black triangle. This is called a pull-down box. If you click on the box a
list of options will appear for you to select from. Each of these options
will take you to a different preference window. Figure 8 lists the categories you have to select from when customizing your browser. This dialog window usually opens to the category you were last modifying, so
don't be disoriented when it looks different each time.

One of the first preferences that you might want to modify is the
location of the web page that is automatically selected and displayed
when you begin a session with your Web browser. If you're working with a
browser that hasn't been customized before, it probably has the opening
web page set to the company that made it. If you're working on one of
your school's computers, then the opening web page may already be set
to the school's page. If you would prefer to begin with another Web page,
the *Appearance* preference window (Figure 9) provides the option to enter

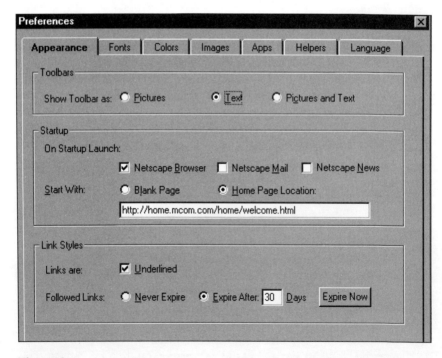

**Figure 9**
Your browser is easily customized to display your toolbar and home page
preferences.

**Figure 10**
Selecting a font of appropriate style and size will help you prevent eye strain and muscle fatigue from leaning over your computer to read.

the Web page of your preference. By now you've probably found something on the Web that you are willing to call home. Enter the URL as illustrated and every time you start your browser or select Home from the toolbar you'll end up at this URL. Later in this chapter you'll see how you can make and display your own home page. Stay tuned. Notice that you also have the option of modifying the appearance of your toolbar.

On the *Appearance* preference window you also have the option of customizing the appearance of your hyperlinks. You've probably noticed that hyperlinks are normally blue (if you or someone else hasn't changed the default color). Once you've accessed them, they change to purple. This follows the bread crumb principle. It lets you know that you've already been down that link and therefore you should select a different path. You can set the length of time for a hyperlink before it changes back to the default color. The default is usually 30 days (Figure 9). Notice that you have the option of having the browser underline the hyperlinks or leave them plain.

If you select the *Fonts* preference window you will see a dialog window (Figure 10) that will allow you to modify the style and size of the text font displayed by your browser. If you typically have a difficult time reading small text from a computer screen, then you may want to increase the size of the font or change it to a style that better suits your needs.

As with fonts, the default text, hyperlink, and background colors can be modified on your browser to reflect the screen conditions you desire (Figure 11). It is important to set the colors to maximize the contrast between text, links, and background. Of course, you may choose to color your text the same color as your hyperlinks just to cause you more chaos in navigating a page.

There are other options available to you for customizing your browser. An extensive explanation is available to you through the *Netscape* Web page. If you are using another browser, you will find that they have similar options and on occasion some browsers may give you more power to control your browser's appearance. Take some time to explore the various options. And again, remember that it's OK to try different settings.

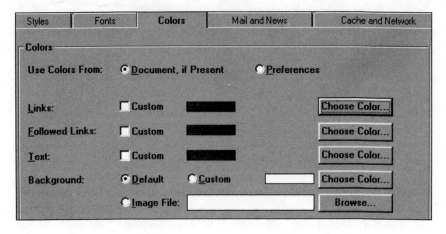

**Figure 11**
Customizing the colors of the components on your browser will help you
quickly identify hyperlinks and navigational paths as you travel.


## 3.2 Do You Get the News Delivered?

One of the tremendous assets of the Web is the access it provides the user.
Using various forms of communication on the Web, one can communicate
with individuals throughout the world. The advantage of using the Web is
the immediacy of communication (no more waiting for weeks for the sur-
face mail) and the ease of sending and receiving communications. Finally,
once you have learned the tools to find an individual or groups of people,
the diversity of those you communicate with can increase to rather dramatic
proportions. Recent advances in Web browsers provide you the opportunity
to communicate through e-mail, newsgroups, and on-line interest groups.

### E-mail

As discussed earlier, e-mail is the electronic exchange of mail among people: from one person to another, or between large groups of people. E-mail
really consists of several elements. At the level of your computer, e-mail is
like a mailbox that allows you to both send and receive messages. At the
level of your service provider, e-mail requires what is analogous to a post
office. To gather and interpret e-mail messages, your service provider
needs to have the ability to interpret a computer protocol called Simple
Mail Transport Protocol (SMTP). The SMTP protocol allows your provider
to not only receive mail, but also to sort it into bundles for individual users.

Access to e-mail can be readily acquired from a commercial service
provider or your educational institution. If you are at a campus that has

provided you with Internet access, you should also have the ability to apply for an e-mail account through your campus computer administration. If you are not provided this access you can also access e-mail through a commercial Internet service provider. In fact, if you've already gone through a service provider for access to the Internet, you probably already have e-mail capabilities. There are several things that you'll need to enter into your mail configuration file. As shown under the *Identity* option under mail preferences (see Figure 12) you will need to enter (1) your name, (2) your e-mail address (this is provided by your service provider), (3) who you want people to reply to when you send them a message (normally you enter your e-mail address here), and (4) the name of your organization or school. Click on OK, then click on the *Server* option on the menu. Again, referring to Figure 12, there are several pieces of information you will need to enter here. First, enter the outgoing mail SMTP server. This is the host name of the server (ask your service provider if you don't know). Second, you will need to enter the POP server name if your service provider does not use an SMTP server. Next, under Pop3 user name, enter your e-mail name only (that's the part before the @ in your e-mail address). That's it! Now you are ready to send and receive mail! No more postage stamps or trips to the post office.

E-mail addresses typically take a very distinctive format. Here is the format of a typical e-mail address: NAME@HOST.DOMAIN. It is not necessary to have a full name for the NAME part of the address and, in fact, some addresses use only numbers to represent an individual. The @ symbol always follows the individual's name, and then comes the name of the mail server computer (HOST). The domain in the e-mail format, just like the domain of the URL format, is used to denote the affiliation of the user. Notice that there are no spaces anywhere in an e-mail address.

E-mail links are built within many Web pages to allow you the opportunity to send a message to the individual listed on the page. Once you click on the e-mail link, your e-mail program will be displayed on

---

If you follow this URL you'll end up on the QualComm homepage where you can download either the free version of *Eudora* or get information on the more powerful commercial version. You can also download a copy of the basic user manual.

### http://www.qualcomm.com/main/contacts.html

The following site by Andrew Starr contains terrific information on how to obtain help when using *Eudora,* and it provides information on how to deal with common set-up problems.

### http://www.amherst.edu/~atstarr/eudora/eudora.html

---

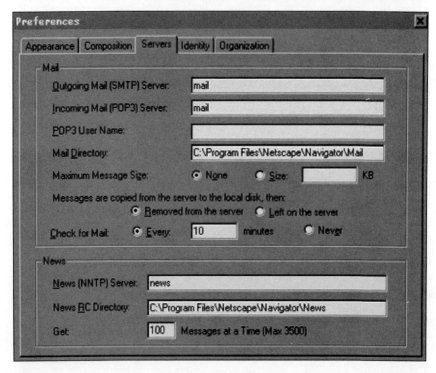

**Figure 12**

Setting up your browser to deal with your e-mail is a rather simple process.
You may need to obtain certain information from your service provider.

your screen with the individual's e-mail address automatically inserted. Simply enter a message and click on the send button. *Netscape* has a very good e-mail program, but if you want to set up to a more sophisticated e-mail program you may want to consider looking at *Eudora*. This program is available for PC's and Mac's and is free. It has some rather powerful features such as the ability to filter or screen certain messages and can send or attach lengthy files in a number of file formats.

---

Here is an example of a typical e-mail address. There are three basic components to a typical e-mail address.

### AStull@biology.fullerton.edu

Here are the three components:
- **individual**   AStull
- **mail server**  biology.fullerton
- **domain**       edu

If you've read the title page to his manual, you'll realize that this is my e-mail address. I may regret putting it here but your comments and suggestions are important. Drop me a brief note if you have some suggestions for making this manual better. (E-mail addresses are not case-sensitive. I use capitals so that addresses are easier to translate.)

---

**Newsgroups**

A second feature incorporated in recent browsers is the ability to exchange ideas over something called Netnews or Newsgroups. A newsgroup is a group of people who connect to and participate in a specialized discussion. These groups are open forums and all are welcome to contribute in the interchange. Some are moderated by an individual or individuals who will post items for discussion and moderate the electronic brawls that ensue. Others are free-form and function much more like a street fight. The bottom line with all newsgroups is to have a central place where people can bring to the table new ideas and perspectives. No, not all newsgroups are places for disagreement.

There are numerous educational newsgroups. Some of the active groups are listed in Appendix III. A good way to begin your journey is to use the newsgroups listed on Internet for Educators (http://www.execpc.com/ ~hughes/usenet.html). Once you find a newsgroup you are interested in examining, simply click on its name and a newsgroup reader will appear. Once in the reader you can read messages, respond to those messages for all to see, post a new message to the group, or respond to the individual who has posted a message by sending that individual an e-mail response that only he or she will receive. As seen from Figure 13, it is rather easy to read, post, and reply to e-mail messages. Note also that newsreaders don't automatically store newsgroups. You will need to enter these by typing in their names. Once you have entered the name of a newsgroup, however, it will automatically appear the next time you use the newsreader—even if you start a new session.

Newsgroups are tremendously rich sites for sharing information, seeking resources, or simply obtaining a sense for the issues being discussed within a certain subject matter area or area of specialization. Don't overlook newsgroups as a means of building professional relationships and networking with your educational colleagues.

---

Here is an example of a typical newsgroup address when using a newsgroup reader. Newsgroup names are divided into several descriptive words separated by a period and organized into a hierarchy.

### K12.chat.teacher

Here are components you will need to enter into your browser's newsgroup reader:

**top category** k12
**sub category** chat
**sub category** teacher

---

The only way to really understand what newsgroups are like is to try them. Here are a couple of newsgroups that will get you started. Connect to one of interest and read some of the postings. You can find a larger list in Appendix III. For your first time, you should just read the postings and follow some of the conversations. Connections or threads develop between postings as people add comments to earlier postings. As you become familiar with the topic of discussion, you might post a comment yourself.

### k12.chat.elementary
### k12.chat.senior
### k12.sys.projects

To get the real flavor of a newsgroup you need to spend more than just a couple of minutes viewing one. Choose a newsgroup of interest. Within that newsgroup select a topic that is being discussed and follow it for a week. As a discussion grows, you'll notice that many people will jump in to participate.

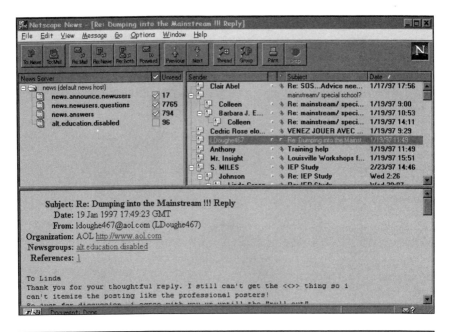

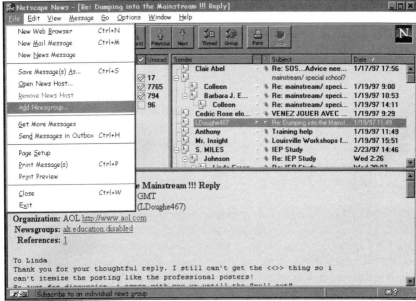

**Figure 13**

Newsreaders are easy to use and allow you the option of viewing posted messages, responding to the message by e-mail, or posting it to the newsgroup, or allowing you to post a new message for the newsgroup.

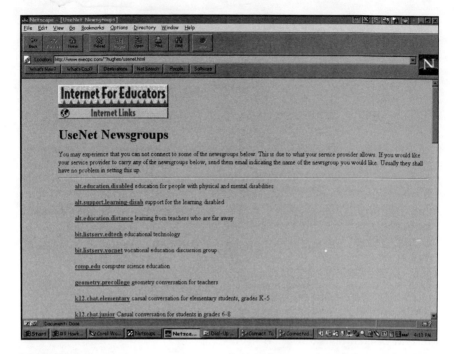

**Figure 14**
*Internet for Educators'* web site provides easy access to numerous educational newsgroups.

## 3.3    Making Your Own Personal Page

Let's get personal on cyberspace. Everyone who has an Internet account can create his or her own personal page containing personal information, links to their favorite Web sites, photos, images, or just about anything else. It is not as simple as browsing the Web *but* it's not very hard either. If your campus has a Web server, then they may have a place for student personal pages. Ask around to see if you are allowed to keep a personal page there. If you can't get access through your campus, you still have other options. Some of the pages that you view on your browser reside on a Web server, but you can also create a file on your home computer or even on a floppy disk that will act as a personal page for you. Admittedly, in order for your personal page to be on the Internet you'd need access to a Web server, but it's not necessary for the basics that I'll describe here. Another option is to use a private service provider to gain access to the Internet. Some service providers rent space to keep home pages on their server. One of the latest things is the idea of the Internet

Coffee House. There are several that have just opened up. They'll serve up great coffee and provide you with access to the Web. Some have even gone as far as renting space for personal pages. Search one out.

## Personal Pages

Personal pages can be rather handy for you or others on the Web. A personal page is a good place to organize and display important sites on the Web. You may, for example, want to list libraries, personal pages of your friends, sites for obtaining information for your hobbies or interests, or sites that allow you to browse recent audio recordings.

Now, where is yours? Actually, I've already made one for you. All you have to do is add the stuff about yourself and the links that you think are cool and interesting. Once you've done that, it's all downhill. If you look at Appendix IV, you'll see that there is a lot of gibberish that may or may not look like computer programming to you. This is the personal page that I've written for you and it's written in HTML. (Remember that HTML is a language that Web browsers use to read hypertext documents.) It's a very simple computer language. In fact, it's so simple that it ranks closer to slang than language. Although this personal page in its present state is quite generic, you'll have plenty of opportunity at the end-of-chapter exercise to liven it up. I don't want you to do anything with it yet. I just want you to see what HTML looks like. We have many basics to discuss before you'll do anything reasonable with it.

---

Just to give you some idea of what other educators and their students have produced for their personal pages, use the following URL:

**http://web66.coled.umn.edu/schools.html**

---

## HTML

The language that you saw on the template home page in Appendix IV is really pretty easy to understand. There are only a couple of things that you need to remember in order to read HTML. If you ignore the HTML symbols that you don't quite understand, you'll see that the rest of the document makes sense. You can do this by alternately viewing your personal page file through your browser and then through your word processor. You don't need a fancy program to write HTML, just a word processor and an understanding of the code. Now look at the page with the HTML language. Notice that HTML typically, but not always, comes in sets of two. At the very top you'll see a tag like this: <HTML>. A *tag* is an element of HTML code. It is added to the page to emphasize the text that will appear on the viewed Web page. Tags always have an angle bracket (<) at the beginning and an opposite angle bracket (>) at the end. Here are a couple of examples: <Body>, <HEAD>, and <TITLE>. The other part of each tag set has a forward slash (/) preceding the word. Here are the other members of the tag pairs: </BODY>, </HEAD>, and </TITLE>. Tags, when used in sets or pairs, surround a section of text and define the beginning and end of an HTML section. Yes, it is possible to use tags incorrectly, just as it is possible to use English incorrectly. Here is an example of the basic HTML page that any properly coded page would conform to.

**<HTML>**
  **<HEAD>**
      This is where a description and purpose of the page is written. The material that is here is not intended to be viewed on the browser. It is only used to document the intent of the page.
  **</HEAD>**
  **<BODY>**
      This is where the material that is to be viewed through the browser will be written.
  **</BODY>**
**</HTML>**

All properly coded HTML documents are coded with this basic format. Notice the beginning and ending member of each tag pair. Although tags usually operate in pairs, some are used as solitary tags. Here are important examples of solitary tags that you should be aware of because they appear in your generic home page. When you want to separate sections of text with two spaces you might use the paragraph tag, <P>. Two line break tags, <BR>, will also do the same thing. If you wanted the browser to make a horizontal line across the viewed page, then you would use a horizontal rule tag, <HR>. If you're paying attention to the tags, you'll notice that the tag names are abbreviations of what they do. Remember, you don't really have to absorb all this language stuff now. I made a link on your personal page that jumps you to several HTML resources.

Many other people have already written cool personal pages and you could use theirs for a template if you don't like the one I wrote. One of the best things about writing HTML is that you really don't have to write it yourself. *Netscape* and many of the other browsers provide a great tool. If you select the *Source . . .* submenu under the *View* menu at the top of your screen, the actual HTML code of the page you are viewing will be displayed for you. All you have to do is find the cool and interesting things that others have done, copy the code, and modify them to reflect your personality.

If you really want to jump into this HTML thing, then here are a number of resources that will help you go further. I have tried to find the resources that will be most beneficial to beginners. Some of these URLs may already be included on the homepage I created for you.

*Web66 SharePages*
This site contains numerous HTML pages, icons, clip art, and flags that can be downloaded and inserted into your HTML documents.

**http://web66.coled.umn.edu/share/share.html**

*HTML: An Interactive Tutorial for Beginners*
This site provides a comprehensive tutorial for HTML beginners. Using a hands-on approach, this site allows you to actually test out your skills as you learn within your browser. This would be an excellent place to start if you want to experience directly the creation of Web pages using HTML.

**http://www.davesite.com/webstation/html**

*HTML Editors—Yahoo!*
Editors are an important tool to reduce the time spent in constructing an HTML document. These editors simplify the construction of HTML by allowing the user to click on buttons or menu items to insert, edit, and paste information. Many editors also have spelling checkers and some even check the syntax of your document. *Yahoo!* has a comprehensive list of editors for PC and Macintosh. Many of these editors have shareware versions that can be downloaded from this site.

**http://www.yahoo.com/computers_and_internet/Internet/World_Wide_Web/html_editors/**

## Hyperlinks

One very important element in HTML is the code for hyperlinks (jumping points within Web pages). You know most of what you need to know to create hyperlinks. The HTML tag for a hyperlink is called an anchor, and it uses the tag pair <A> and </A>. There are two main components to an anchor tag. The first element is the URL and the second is the word. Here is an example of an anchor tag:

```
<A HREF="URL">
  Word
</A>
```

This is a little more than the <A> and </A> that I described earlier but it's still not that hard. I'll dismantle it for you and you can see how it works. The first line of the example above begins the code for an anchor. Notice again the <A>, but also notice that there is a lot more garbage thrown in between the A and the last angle bracket. You should also notice that this garbage is a URL. This URL tells the browser the location of the requested document. The second line is the text as it will appear on the HTML page (the button, so to speak). Because it will be a hypertext link, it will appear as a colored link by your browser. The anchor tag set is completed with the ending anchor tag, </A>. As it operates on an actual Web page, if the user selects the hypertext link, then the user will be sent the document specified by the URL.

Now for an exercise. Use your word processor and type in the basic page elements that I gave to you earlier (<HTML> and </HTML>). Within the body of the page I want you to type in an anchor tag set using a real URL. Use one or both of the examples provided below. Once you have this page, save it with the name TEST.HTML and view it with your browser.

**A Beginner's Guide to HTML**
  **http://www.ncsa.uiuc.edu/General/Internet/WWW/**
  **HTMLPrimer.html**
**How to Publish on the Web**
  **http://www.thegiim.org/**

See step 2 in the following section for help in finding and displaying this file. Once you've got this page up and running on your browser, try the hyperlink. Does it work? You should notice that these URLs will take you to resources that will tell you more about Web publishing.

## Home

So, you have a personal page. Where do you put it to make it work? Well, this depends on whether you will have access to a Web server or not. I'll assume that you don't and give you some instructions that will still help you use it to your advantage. Once you've completed your personal page, you'll have a file on either your hard drive or a floppy disk. The advantage of having your home page on floppy disk is that you'll have a portable home page that you can use on any computer. I'll give you a five-step procedure for finding and setting your default home page to the one you've created.

1. *After* you have finished the end-of-chapter exercise, you should copy your personal page to either a floppy disk or your hard drive.
2. With *Netscape* you should notice that there is a command under the *File* menu called *Open File . . .* . If you initiate this command, you'll get a dialog window where you can designate the file you wish to open. The trick to this is that this file isn't on a server. Select the HTML file from either your floppy drive or hard drive and press the Return key on your keyboard. Because your file is written in HTML your browser will open up and display it for you.
3. If it isn't set already, change your *Options* setting so that you can view the URLs of the pages that display on your browser. When this is set properly, you'll notice that your file's URL is listed something like this: file:///. . . . . . . . . . . ./file.html. Notice that the protocol is not HTTP and that you may have more than two slashes.
4. Record this URL on a piece of paper so that you can refer to it in the next step. I would ask you to remember it and copy it to step 5, but every little slash and colon is important. So, this will save you from a possible SNAFU (Situation Normal. All Fouled Up. I learned this from a friend in the Army).
5. If you remember from earlier in this chapter, I described how you can change the home page designation for your browser. Go back to this section and use the description to open the *Preferences* section of the *Options* menu. Open the preference for *Windows* and *Links* and enter the URL that you wrote down from step 4 into the home page entry window.

Now that you've performed these steps, your browser should automatically jump you onto your home page when you select the Home button from the toolbar. Give it a try. The procedures that you've just performed have allowed your browser to memorize the location of your personal page file. If you move it or erase it, then you'll have to do this all over again. Builds character—right?

## For Those Who Don't Want to Use HTML

It really isn't necessary that you use HTML to make your own personal page or, for that matter, to create a comprehensive Web site. During the past year a plethora of software programs called Web authors have come on the market. These are really wonderful programs because they allow you to create a Web page in a manner very similar to creating a document on a word processor. In fact, the latest versions of Corel's *WordPerfect* and Microsoft's *Word* both allow you to create Web pages from within the program. And you will never have to see any HTML!!

A personal page created in 5 minutes using WordPerfect 7.0's Web tool is shown in Figure 15. Note that it has links, a wallpaper background, and even an e-mail link so someone can click on your name and send you an immediate e-mail message. And all this took 5 minutes to create!! If you're interested in learning more about these authoring tools, check out *Yahoo!*'s review of various authoring tools (http://www.yahoo.com) by doing a search on Web authoring tools.

• • • • • • • •
## Activity

### Make Yourself at Home!
The activity of the day is to make your personal page with bookmarks. One of the greatest problems that I have, as a teacher and administrator of a student network, is the gradual and insidious buildup of cluttersome

**Figure 15**
This is a personal page created by using WordPerfect 7.0's Web tool.

bookmarks. The situation is obvious: Each student changes the browsers on the computers in my classroom to meet his or her personal needs. I never know what to expect when I need to teach a class or use a browser. Students, with much less experience, are confused and disoriented. I have, to some extent, come up with a solution.

The HTML that you will see in Appendix IV is my solution. It is a template for a student home page to be kept on a floppy disk. The added value in this is that you can also use this generic home page as a portable resource disk on most networked computers. The only drawback is that you can't jump between Macintosh and Windows with this arrangement. But then, I'll leave that up to the computer giants.

You should know a couple of conventions so that you will understand what you need to do. I have used a *large italic font* to represent the text that you are to replace with your information. HTML tags are represented in a <SMALLER FONT, ALL IN UPPER-CASE AND WITH ANGLE BRACKETS>. Text that is not an HTML tag and *does not* need to be changed is in a regular size and font.

To create a homepage on a floppy disk, simply use any word processor to type the following information onto a floppy disk. Give the file a name with the suffix html (HOMENAME.HTML). Once this is done, you should follow the instructions in section 3.3 to adapt it to your liking. Remember to show some style and personality!

# Glossary
# It's All Greek to Me

• • • • • • •

*Archie*    This is a search tool used to find resources that are stored on Internet-based FTP servers. Contrary to what I said earlier in the manual, Archie is short for Archive because it performs an archive search for resources. (See FTP and Server)

**AVI**    This stands for Audio/Video Interleaved. It is a Microsoft Corporation format for encoding video and audio for digital transmission.

**Background**    This refers to an image or color that is present in the background of a viewed Web document. Complex images are becoming very popular as backgrounds but require a great deal more time to download. The color of default background can be set for most Web browsers.

**Bookmark**    This refers to a list of URLs saved within a browser. The user can edit and modify the bookmark list to add and delete URLs as the user's interests change. Bookmark is a term used by *Netscape* to refer to the user's list of URLs, while 'Hotlist' is used by *Mosaic* to refer to the same list. (See Hotlist, *Mosaic,* and URL)

**Browser**    This is a software program that is used to view and browse information on the Internet. Browsers are also referred to as clients. (See Client)

**Bulletin Board Service**    This is an electronic bulletin board. It is sometimes referred to as a BBS. Information on a BBS is posted to a computer where many can dial in and read it and/or comment on it. BBSs may or may not be connected to the Internet. Some are accessible by modem dial-in only.

**Cache**    This refers to a section of memory that is set aside to store information that is commonly used by the computer or an active piece of software. Most browsers will create a cache of commonly accessed images. An example might be the images that are common to the user's homepage. Retrieving images from the cache is much quicker than downloading the images from the original source each time they are required.

**Clickable image (Clickable map)**    This refers to an interface used in Web documents that allows the user to click or select different areas of an image and receive different responses. Clickable images are becoming very common as a way of offering a user many different selections within a common visual format.

**Client**    This is a software program used to view information from remote computers. Clients function in a Client-Server information exchange model. This term may also be loosely applied to the computer that is used to request information from the server. (See Server)

**Compressed file**    This refers to a file or document that has been compacted to save memory space so that it can be easily and quickly transferred through the Internet.

**Download**    This is the process of transferring a file, document, or program from a remote computer to a local computer. (See Upload)

**E-mail**    This is the short name for electronic mail. E-mail is sent electronically from one person to another. Some companies have e-mail systems that are not part of the Internet. E-mail can also be sent to one person or to many different people. I sometimes refer to this as JunkE-mail. You form your own opinions.

**FAQ**    This stands for Frequently Asked Questions. An FAQ is a file or document where a moderator or administrator will post commonly asked questions and their answers. Although it is very easy to communicate across the Internet, if you have a question, you should check for the answer in an FAQ first.

**Forms**    This refers to an interface element used within Web documents to allow a user to send information back to a Web server. With a forms interface, the user is requested to type responses within entry windows to be returned to the server for processing. Forms rely on a server computer to process the submittals. They are becoming more common as browser and server software improve.

**FTP**    This stands for File Transfer Protocol. It is a procedure used to transfer large files and programs from one computer to another. Access to the computer to transfer files may or may not require a password. Some FTP servers are set up to allow public access by anonymous log-on. This process is referred to as *Anonymous FTP.*

**GIF**    This stands for Graphics Interchange Format. It is a format created by CompuServe to allow electronic transfer of digital images. GIF files are a common format and can be viewed by both Mac and Windows users.

*Gopher*    This is a format structure and resource for providing information on the Internet. It was created at the University of Minnesota.

**GUI**    An acronym for Graphical User Interface. It is a combination of the appearance and the method of interacting with a computer. A

GUI requires the use of a mouse to select commands on an icon-based monitor screen. Macintosh and Windows operating systems are typical GUI examples.

**Homepage**   In its specific sense, this refers to a Web document that a browser loads as its central navigational point to browse the Internet. It may also be used to refer to a Web page describing an individual. In the most general sense, it is used to refer to any Web document.

**Hotlist**   This is a list of URLs saved within the *Mosaic* Web browser. This same list is referred to as a Bookmark within the *Netscape* Web browser.

**HTML**   An abbreviation for HyperText Markup Language, the common language used to write documents that appear on the World Wide Web.

**HTTP**   An abbreviation for HyperText Transport Protocol, the common protocol used to communicate between World Wide Web servers.

**Hypertext**   This refers to text elements within a document that have an embedded connection to another item. Web documents use hyper-text links to access documents, images, sounds, and video files from the Internet. The term hyperlink is a general term that applies to elements on Web pages other than text.

**Inline image**   This refers to images that are viewed along with text on Web documents. All inline images are in the GIF format. JPEG format is the other common image format for Web documents, but an external viewer is typically required to view them.

**JPEG**   This stands for Joint Photographic Experts Group. It is also commonly used to refer to a format used to transfer digital images.

***Jughead***   This is a service for performing searches on the Internet. (see *Archie* and *Veronica*)

***Mosaic***   This is the name of the browser that was created at the National Center for Supercomputing Applications. It was the first Web browser to have a consistent interface for the Macintosh, Windows, and UNIX environments. The success of this browser is really responsible for the expansion of the Web.

**MPEG**   This stands for Motion Picture Experts Group. It is also a format used to make, view, and transfer both digital audio and digital video files.

**Newsgroup**   This is the name for the discussion groups that can be on the Usenet. Not all newsgroups are accessible through the Internet. Some are accessible only through a modem connection.

**QuickTime**   This is a format used by Apple Computer to make, view, edit, and send digital audio and video.

**Server**   This is a software program used to provide, or serve, information to remote computers. Servers function in a Client-Server information exchange model. This term may also be loosely applied to the computer that is used to serve the information. (See Client)

**Table**   This refers to a specific formatting element found in HTML pages. Tables are used on HTML documents to organize information visually.

**Telnet**   This is the process of remotely connecting and using a computer at a distant location.

**Upload**   This is the process of moving or transferring a document, file, or program from one computer to another computer.

**URL**   This is an abbreviation for Uniform Resource Locator. In its basic sense it is an address used by people on the Internet to locate documents. URLs take a common format that describes the protocol for information transfer, the host computer address, path to the desired file, and the name of the file requested.

**Usenet**   This is a worldwide system of discussion groups, also called newsgroups. There are many thousand newsgroups, but only a percentage are accessible from the Internet.

***Veronica***   Believe it or not, this is an acronym. It stands for Very Easy Rodent Oriented Net-wide Index to Computerized Archives. This is a database of menu names from a large number of *Gopher* servers. It is a quick and easy way to search *Gopher* resources for information by keyword. It was developed at the University of Nevada.

**WAIS**   This stands for Wide Area Information Servers. This is a software package that allows the searching of large indexes of information from the Internet.

**WAV**   This stands for Waveform sound format. It is a Microsoft Corporation format for encoding sound files.

**Web (WWW)**   This stands for the World Wide Web. When loosely applied, this term refers to the Internet and all of its associated incarnations such as *Gopher,* FTP, HTTP, etc. More specifically, this term refers to a subset of the servers on the Internet that use HTTP to transfer hyperlinked documents in a page-like format.

# Appendix I
# What's Under the Hood?

•••••••

## *Basic Components*

Here is a computer question to get your mind working. What is the difference between a Corvette and a Chevette? Okay, it's a stupid question but give it some consideration. The difference is a couple thousand dollars. Everything else is just fluff, mileage, and auto insurance. But if we break this down to our basic needs (if we really need a ride), both cars are the same. The same goes for computers and networks. The simple no-gloss stuff will get you by while saving you money; and the high-gloss stuff will transform your cash into dash and make your Internet browsing a little more enjoyable. Many of you may be lucky enough to have computers on your campus that are set up to allow Internet access. In case you don't, I'll list the *minimum* systems, connections, and services that you'll need to enter the Internet, but you'll have to decide how shiny your system needs to be.

### The Computer

Now watch how you approach this issue if you ask for advice on which computer platform to buy. Opinions are known to run a little hot with some people when they begin to argue the differences between Macintosh and PC-compatible systems. Proponents from both camps can easily get out of hand. If they begin to foam at the mouth, then you know you're in for a real adventure. The best advice that I can give to you is test them both at a computer store. Choose the one that you can pay for and are most comfortable using. After all, it won't do you any good if you don't enjoy using it or if it gets repossessed halfway through the semester.

These are the **minimum** system configurations that you'll need.

*Macintosh*
68020
System 7.0

*PC-Compatible*
Intel 486
Windows 3.1

51

| 256 color monitor | VGA monitor |
| 16 MB of RAM | 16 MB of RAM |
| 15 MB of disk space | 15 MB of disk space |

## The Internet Connection

If you get lucky, your university has already recognized the importance of the Internet as a teaching and learning tool. If the equipment is set up, then it should have Internet, or more specifically, Web access ready to go. Okay, if you didn't enroll in a school campus with vision, bucks, or both, then you'll have to do it the hard way. There are many resources that can help you set up a connection from home.

Some campuses, although lacking a walk-in lab, have made arrangements for students to dial into the campus computer system and hopefully the Internet with a modem. If such is the case, then search out the campus computer hack and ask for help. This may require a fair amount of begging, bribing, or borrowing.

Another option for accessing the Internet is to subscribe to a company such as American Online, CompuServe, Prodigy, or Microsoft. Many other companies are also in business to sell you access to the Internet and you should consider them in addition to these. Some of these on-line service providers advertise the availability of access. However, you are required to use their software and it may not have all of the options that you might want. As always, it is a buyer's market and you should shop around and test drive everything before you buy.

When it comes to buying modems, I suggest you buy a 56.6K baud modem. A baud is a measure of the speed with which the modem transfers data. The higher the number, usually the faster the transfer rate. With a typical 56.6K baud modem you can expect that it will take a few seconds to transfer a typical Web page, but this will vary depending on the complexity of the page.

## The Browser Software

If everything has fallen into place, you should now have access to a computer with muscle and a gateway to the Internet, either through your school or an Internet service provider. But you're missing one very important piece, the Web client software. A more descriptive name for this software is *browser*, as that is what most people do with it. It is used to browse or wander, sometimes aimlessly, through the Internet.

There are many Web browsers on the market, and in the space of time that it has taken me to write this manual, I would not doubt that several more have entered the race to capture your dollar. The mother of all browsers is *Netscape Navigator,* now in version 3.01, but there are a number of other browsers available. You should really evaluate them all and choose the one that you're most comfortable with. Browsers are typically very cheap, if not simply free for educational use. (Considering the nature of my audience, I should give proper reverence to that last statement.) *Netscape, Mosaic,* and many of the other browsers are FREE for student use! So, don't be afraid to evaluate them all.

Now, if you have all of these basic elements and they've been put together correctly, you should be ready to surf! Enjoy!

# Appendix II
# A Call to Order
• • • • • • •
## *Internet Providers*

*America Online*
American Online Inc.
8619 Westwood Center Dr.
Vienna, VA 22182-2285
800-827-6364
703-448-8700
aohotline@aol.com

*CompuServe*
CompuServe Inc.
5000 Arlington Centre Blvd.
Columbus, OH 43220
800-487-9197
614-457-8600
70006.101@compuserve.com

*Prodigy*
Prodigy Services Co.
445 Hamilton Ave.
White Plains, NY 10601
800-776-3449

If you don't want to use one of these large service providers but would prefer a company that drops the frills and gives you direct access to the Internet, you can locate such service providers at this Web address:

**(http://www.celestin.com/pocia/)**

Just search by the area code for your phone service and you'll get a list of providers that will accept your money to use their service.

# Appendix III
# All the News That's Fit to Be Webbed

•••••••

*Education Newsgroups*

Think of this as a starter kit to education groups on the Usenet. This is not a complete list and some of the newsgroups that I've listed will, without a doubt, disappear in the near future. Additionally, there will be many new groups born in this same time period. One of them might even be yours. As I've said before, it's a changing world.

The names are very descriptive for the topic of discussion. You will find that some are very interesting and some are not. Subscribe to several of the groups and eavesdrop on their conversations for awhile before you jump in. This will give you some experience with the general attitude of the group and prevent some embarrassment on your part. I also suggest that you read the FAQ and any postings directed to new participants to the group.

**k12.chat.elementary** casual conversation for elementary students grades K–5.

**k12.chat.junior** casual conversation for students in grades 6–8.

**k12.chat.senior** casual conversation for high school students.

**k12.chat.teacher** casual conversation for teachers of grades K–12.

**k12.ed.art** arts and crafts curricula in K–12 education.

**k12.ed.business** business education curricula in grades K–12.

**k12.ed.comp.literacy** teaching computer literacy in grades K–12.

**k12.ed.health-pe** health and physical education curricula in grades K–12.

**k12.ed.life-skills** home economics, career education, and school counseling.

**k12.ed.math** mathematics curriculum in K–12 education.

**k12.ed.music** music education and performing arts curriculum in grades K–12.

**k12.ed.science** science curriculum for grades K–12.

**k12.ed.soc-studies** geography, civics, political science, and history curriculum for K–12.

**k12.ed.special** education of students with special needs.

**k12.ed.tag** K–12 curriculum for gifted and talented students.

**k12.ed.tech** industrial arts and vocational education.

**k12.lang.art** language arts (reading, writing, literature) instruction.

**k12.lang.deutsch-eng** bilingual German/English practice with native speakers.

**k12.lang.esp-eng** bilingual Spanish/English practice with native speakers.

**k12.lang.francais** French practice with native speakers.

**k12.lang.russian** bilingual Russian/English practice with native speakers.

**k12.library** implementing information technology in school libraries.

**k12.sys.ch0(through ch12)** current projects.

**k12.sys.projects** potential projects.

# Appendix V
# Stepping Out

• • • • • • •

*Student Homepage Template*

```
<HTML>
<HEAD>
  <TITLE>Your Home Page</TITLE>
</HEAD>

<BODY>
<CENTER>
  <H1>Your Name</H1>
  <H2>Your Title, Major, or Philosophy</H2>
  <H3>
  <ADDRESS>
    Your address<BR>
    May<BR>
    Go<BR>
    Here<BR>
    <P>
    Your e-mail address<BR>
  </ADDRESS>
  </H3>
</CENTER>
<HR>

<DL>
  <H2>This Is Your Life:</H2>
  <DD>Just say something about yourself. After you've
  added something to your homepage file compare it to
```

*what actually shows on your browser. You'll notice that most of this gibberish is not visible.*

`<P>`

`<DD>`*You can have as many paragraphs as you wish. Here's another. Enjoy.*

`<P>`

`</DL>`

`<DL>`

   `<H2>`Important Educational Resources`</H2>`

   `<DD>`

      `<A HREF="http://www.execpc.com/~hughes">`
      Internet for Educators Resources

      `</A>`

`</DL>`

`<HR>`

`<DL>`

   `<H2>`Handbooks and Manuals`</H2>`

   `<DD>`

      `<A HREF="http://www.matisse.net/files/glossary.html">`
      Glossary of Internet Terms

      `</A>`

   `<DD>`

      `<A HREF="http://www.cdtl.umn.edu/eudora_http/contents.html">`
      Eudora Manual

      `</A>`

   `<DD>`

      `<A HREF="http://home.netscape.com/eng/mozilla/1.1/handbook/">`
      Netscape Handbook

      `</A>`

`</DL>`

`<HR>`

`<DL>`

   `<H2>`Directories and Search Engines:`</H2>`

   `<DD>`

      `<A HREF="http://flosun.salk.edu/cusi.html">`
      CUSI Search Clearinghouse

      `</A>`

```
<DD>
    <A HREF="http://altavista.digital.com/">
    AltaVista Search Engine
    </A>
<DD>
    <A HREF="http://www.yahoo.com/">
    Yahoo Directory
    </A>
</DL>
<HR>
<DL>
    <H2>Design and Publish:</H2>
    <DD>
        <A HREF="http://www.ncsa.uiuc.edu/General/Internet/WWW
        /HTMLPrimer.html">
        A Beginner's Guide to HTML
        </A>
    <DD>
        <A HREF="http://www.access.digex.net/~werbach
        /barebone.html">
        The BareBones Guide to HTML
        </A>
    <DD>
        <A HREF="http://www.thegiim.org/">
        How to Publish On The Web
        </A>
</DL>
<HR>
<H3>
        Your Name<A HREF="mailto:Name@server.edu">E-mail
        address</A>
</H3>

</BODY>
</HTML>
```